*

the stars, your eyes

*

*

the stars, your eyes

*

terry s. johnson

SHANTI ARTS PUBLISHING

BRUNSWICK, MAINE

the stars, your eyes

Published by Shanti Arts Publishing

Designed by Shanti Arts Designs

Shanti Arts LLC
193 Hillside Road
Brunswick, Maine 04011
shantiarts.com

Cover image— joe-pohle / 5XSplbkT2SM / unsplash.com

Printed in the United States of America

ISBN: 978-1-971191-01-0 (softcover)

Contents

Acknowledgments

The author wishes to thank the editors of the following journals
  where these poems first found a home:

Alaska Women Speak: "Fledgling"

Cirque Journal: "Firmament"

Loss, Vol. 9 of the *Lifespan* Series (Pure Slush): "Aftermath's
  Beginning"

Monterey Poetry Review: "Astronomy" (winner of the 2023 Alaska
  Writers' Guild poetry competition) and "Substance"

Passager: "Late Winter, Early Spring"

Raven's Perch: "Grace Bay Villanelle"

The Wild Word: "Dialysis Before Daybreak"; "The Sentence";
  and "Shifting Beach"

The Sentence

Now we know. Was it going to be
your bone marrow producing too
many red cells or your pancreas
failing to produce enough insulin?

We linger in bed after the alarm,
converse about politics, our country
fracturing. Or about climate change
as refugees roam for food and shelter,

which we have always taken for granted.
We skirt your treatment until we can no
longer ignore the doctor's decree—dialysis.
Banished from our known world, you

shall be chained to a machine, a glorious
detention, offering a fragile future.
Even with our many blessings, we want
more. To be human is to be so greedy.

We must create a new lexicon,
shape our denouement.

Harbor

My beloved receives a glossy brochure
describing his upcoming treatment.
We try to understand the diagrams, trace
the blood's dizzying passages yet lose
our way. Diverging paths, dead ends.
A surgeon must form an entry point,
a *fistula*. Latin for panpipes, ancient flutes
fashioned from woody reeds. Breathe
tonguing tunes for banquets, funerals.
I remember my infant daughter, safe
in her car seat, facing her first long tunnel
through a high mountain. The whites
of her eyes widened in fear and wonder,
the dim opening allowing travel otherwise
impossible. *Fistula*, the fusing of an artery
to a vein. We, too, begin in fear, soon marvel
that as one part of the body fails, another
provides the prospect of more time. Next
week, the procedure. Months of healing
before dialysis cleanses dark channels,
shelters the blood's delicate cargo.

Shifting Beach

Even with his back to me, wading
knee deep in the morning's
soft waves, I sense erosion.

He says he's losing pounds
on purpose, but I know this is not
true. He has that look of decline.

Sunken shoulders arch forward. Skin,
taut from the top of the arm, sluices
across a newly-formed ravine below

the sudden rise to brittle clavicle.
He's tired more often, walks more
slowly. In small tremors, his body opens

to deepening faults. My genteel mother
always taught me not to dwell on bodily
functions. It's not polite conversation.

But you and I, my love, are past the realm
of the superficial. We must face the surge
of stark truth. Your kidneys sustained

your bay of blood as long as possible.
Returning home, we close our
eyes, conjure aquamarine

and the sound of surf swelling,
the sea forever changing.
We have shared gold.

Grace Bay Villanelle

Emerging waves against a shore must break
defined by wind and distance from the moon
while humans meander a mysterious fate.

Our unmapped lives a challenge to navigate
through snowstorm, earthquake and typhoon.
Rising waves against a shore must break.

We start and stop, too oft our course waylaid.
Our toil for naught, our efforts like dust strewn.
We humans wander to our unknown fate.

As lovers, we succumb or hesitate,
eventual surrender, torrential swoon.
Soaring waves against a shore must break.

We nurture children, hope and pray
they survive disasters, remain immune.
We humans struggle to our ultimate fate.

If fortunate, a long life can we embrace.
First fight, then accept our nascent decrepitude.
Mounting waves against a shore must break.
We humans collapse to certain fate.

Nighttime

September 11th

You're a bit more comfortable, resting
in bed, watching your favorite sport.
Tennis shots metronome your time.
Never mind your favorite player's usual
finesse. Too many points surrendered,
his match lost.

In another room, I'm watching
an epic set in Nazi-occupied France,
a few years before my own father
flew missions over Italy. I let
the language embrace me, pretend
we can travel still.

The terrors of their days, the world gone mad.
The horrors of ours, generations later.

Held in siege by our new routine,
we missed today's TV tributes.
We tracked food intake, injections,
bathroom going, as you Hindus say.
I did not log the bountiful kisses,
our Kama Sutra. Sustenance against
the enemy at the gates.

Dialysis Before Daybreak

We join scant others on backroads. Most cars carry
one driver. We carry each other, at least for now.

Stars fleck the fading midnight blue as Venus, low
in the sky, kisses the rim of the mountains' face.

Two days ago, a fire roared on the distant range, thick
fog dispersed an eerie glow, seeping between maple

branches edging the asphalt. Is someone
hurt? Are the flames spreading? Last week,

torrential rains each trip, windshield wipers
clicking in too quick a tempo. Soon winter

will snarl its frigid presence in a fury of sleet
and snow. What if I can't get you to the center?

No one has prepared us. No one has prepared us for much
of anything in this throbbing dance of needles and tubes

taunting your flesh, pulsing your poisoned blood
through a rinse cycle. Horrifying, miraculous.

You have dozed off again. I'm comforted by
your breath. Slow, steady. Music of our sphere.

Days On, Days Off

He treats dialysis like a day at the office,
primps to look his best, packs a pristine
magazine in his briefcase, assures me he
can drive by himself. I learn later, little
is read. His nurses report he sleeps despite
the center's cacophony. Once home,
he crashes in bed. On days off, he has
more energy, and I'm conscripted as ball
girl courtside. The machine-launched
yellow orbs set a rhythm of reassuring
predictability. Then we rally, hit balls
back and forth. I haven't played tennis
in decades. *We could have been doing
this together for years*, he exclaims.
Lost opportunities, past and future,
haunt our present. Sometimes, we walk
the bike path. He challenges himself
to three miles. Two is realistic. He even
suggests we eat out, raise a glass
of prosecco, toast today's reprieve.

Ides of March

A lone sparrow sings as if it's spring
as light snow falls. Fierce winds
have diminished, and I can almost
sense the push of bulbs upward,
prospect of sky-blue Siberian scilla
rising in the midst of gray despair.

Or am I just soothing myself? That
this dismal season will end, that you
will miraculously heal, live a bit
longer to experience the earth's
greening in all its imperfect splendor?
How a common bird trilling its lungs out
can provide such comfort?

Late Winter, Early Spring

I'm keeping a window open, hoping the brisk
evening air will purify our home. Phantom whiffs

of leftover stews, sour sweaters, sad conversations.
Birds are returning or perhaps never left.

I'm only now hearing their celebrations, their laments.
I notice the huge oaks, their budding branches

rise like hands in supplication. Their coarse bark
brushed in bright rose from the sunset's reflection.

I'm ready for spring as my beloved prepares
for dying, and so I am preparing, too.

We can't believe we're at the end of our cycle,
our last season together. We're turning a bit

cranky, snipping for the first time. It is not
beautiful, not tulips blooming, but we understand.

Why does it take impending
death to teach the final lesson?

Our life together has been a feast.
One of us will live on in famine.

He's finished his shower. In swoon of aftershave,
I kiss his smooth face, revel in his flesh.

April in Two Landscapes

The gently curved New England ridge
suggests a reclining woman in a verdant
silk robe—paletted in pink redbuds,
white dogwoods, sunrise yellow forsythia.
Waves of blooms, flows of fragrance.

With lightning speed, spring passes.
With a sudden shift, you now gravely ill.

This same month years ago, we celebrated
Seville's *feria*, astonished by *jacaranda*
trees in purple-blue inflorescence.

Women heel-clicked the cobbled streets
in flamenco flamboyance, arm in arm
with their proud men in tight-tailored
black suits. We joined the roar toward
the *Maestranza* for the evening's *corrida*.

Trumpets tossed each bull into the ring.
In taut twenty minute spectacles, life's
struggle rendered—confusion, defiance,
persistence, resignation, defeat.

Satin and sequins, dazzling
distractions to blood oozing.
Red, the truest primal color.

What a man, that bull!
What a bull, that man!

Zürich

He insists we get his passport photo taken right after
his long overdue haircut. I have to admit, he remains
so handsome. He dreams of the Alps, having never
traveled there. Imagines fresh morning air, pure
snow, azure skies, wildflowers in bloom. No! No!
Those are my dreams. He longs for a soft bed
with ironed sheets, for a view of Alpine peaks,
for the sodium pentobarbital that will cease
his pain once he completes the legalities
of assisted dying. He's suffering like Job.
He could tolerate dialysis a bit longer
if it wasn't for the incessant itching
from head to toe. He wills himself
through each long hour, stubborn
as a thorny cactus. But he is, oh,
so tired. Baths, salves, prayers
useless. He no longer wants
to endure. I imagine the day.
I'll whisper in his ear, caress
his still full lips. Wait,
wait. Then leave
the room
alone.

Stay of Execution

i.

Routine liver biopsy.
Bombshell bleed out.
An IV tangle of tubes
armor his body. Neck,
groin, both arms. Time
ticked, drip by drip.

Sudden code blue,
his body limp.
A crash cart
grazes my hip
as I'm escorted out.

Later, I'm allowed
to join him. Monitors
punctuate his few words.
Why are the gods
giving me what . . .
I cannot bear?

His heart stops, again.
Pushed to the wall,
I watch four nurses
perform heroics in practiced
maneuvers.

ii.

Incredibly, he's rescued
a second time, is promoted
to a ward upstairs.

Confinement of routine
boredom, utter fear, deep
appreciation. His daughters
and I take turns at his bedside.

It hurts to eat, so he doesn't.
His stomach's distended
from the IV liquids
that saved him.
Sleep captures more
of his hours each day.

When he does awaken,
he pushes food away.
I'm dying . . . Let me rest . . .
along the way.

After two weeks,
he accepts defeat.
Death . . . the ultimate
joke . . . Here one day . . .
then . . . gone.
I take him home.

Discomfort

Too late for the mountains of Zürich,
we arrange for hospice at home. He
wants to leave his pain behind, impatient

as a little boy awaiting a long promised prize.
The intake counselor assures him the meds
are delivered quickly once dialysis ends.

A few dawns hence, he declares he's done.
His daughters wonder, *Is this it?*
They arrive at noon with the grandkids.

Everyone's on cliff's edge. His youngest
asks that all his possessions be returned.
We must maintain our Hindu heritage.

I wonder if mere belongings can ensure
cultural identity? *It's not the time,* I snap.
The magma of her disrespect

chokes the atmosphere. Ashes color
me villain. His eldest daughter remains
silent. When the nurse arrives, she

senses the air electric, cries with me
when I accompany her outside. *Remember,*
you and John have loved each other dearly.

Substance

Illness quakes your ravaged body.
I try to scaffold your failing body.

Remember the first time we made love?
Ignoring how age had weathered each other's body?

Scars, thinning hair, fissured teeth, didn't matter.
So rapturous to quarry each other's body.

Rivulets gushed between cracks, quenched our thirst.
An offering to find shelter in the caves of each other's body.

Soon I'll receive well-meaning cards. Crystallized
memory will strengthen my heart, my devastated body.

Last Performance

I pretend to run errands, give his family
time without me. The grandkids
have been drawing colorful posters
and practicing songs. They've always
enjoyed entertaining us. I learn later
in snippets what transpired. L did her
rendition of "Let it go." *Conceal, don't feel.*
N breakdanced, ball cap backwards,
oozing cool. Granddaughter M drew
a huge tree with majestic branches
in full foliage. Her quote read,
Even if one leaf falls, the tree grows.
As the husbands packed up the kids to take
them home, I hear one child humming
from the hit *Hamilton, the unimaginable.*

Astronomy

Life withdraws
from his body
despite inherent refusal

A yellow light turns
a slowing down
treatments vetoed

He imagines a different
declination, standing
on the celestial equator

as the universe expands
in all directions. He chooses
a far-flung galaxy,

wills his ashes
to a distant point,
joins a stellar nursery

Time measured
by degrees, minutes,
seconds

Aftermath's Beginning

i.

We wash the body, learn
to dress dead weight, wrestle
to pull on his favorite shirt.
Frame his face with fresh
flowers. Call his sister
in Mumbai, share
a Hindu blessing.

After dark, the nurse signs
the death certificate. She
leaves as his daughters flee.
The chaos of dying done.

I stroke his cooling
lips, his arms, his hands.
Katydids, crickets accompany
this hush of loss.

Late evening, the hearse
arrives. Two old duffers, both
gasping for breath, struggle
with the stretcher, a sweaty
slapstick in summer heat.
They cover him with a hospice
quilt. A red, white and blue
extravaganza. As a naturalized
citizen, he would have chuckled
at such patriotic display.

ii.

Next morning, D-Day plus
one. Deceased Day. Dismal
Day. Day of turbulent weather.
Inundation of death's dreary
bureaucracy, duties filled
with despair. Phone calls, forms,
followed by the frenzy of sorting,
cleaning, packing up. The list
grows like cells dividing.

A storm swirls a tornado
in my heart. Tasks delay
the crush of grief. D-Day
plus two, plus three.
My new eternity.

Distress Intolerance Diagnosed

The shouting, the bitterness,
so unlike you, John. Your body
failing . . . but you insisted . . . you
had failed your body. Time trimmed,
truncated, timed out. The devils
of diabetes attacked with persistent
wrath, declared victory over your soul.
The soles of your feet fragile. With each
painful step, your cells shutting down.
Body as prison, fear of endless internment.
You begged and begged and I, of course,
agreed, to help you escape, carefully
following a doctor-friend's instructions.
Hospice drugs sufficient when dosed
properly. How much lorazepam, how much
morphine, atropine. Rhymes punctuate
your pain. Jack be nimble, Jack be quick,
Jack jump over that damned candlestick.
We didn't voice our love enough
at the end. You, exhausted from dying,
and me, exhausted from taking care.
So many loved ones coming and going.
Our moments alone limited.
Our cherishment assumed.
How fortunate we were until . . .
Well . . . Oh, god . . . I want
to hear your deep voice . . .
Now . . . again and again. You
declared we'd take each other
home. How absurd I thought!
Someone is always left behind.
Yet I knew what you meant.

We would be together
as long as we could, until your
last rasp . . . I, quick. You, now
dead. Grief, memory's echo
chamber . . . And yes!
I am intolerant of this loss . . .
this deafening solitude . . .
bereft.

In Between

All winter I imagined
your impending death, a counterfeit practice.

Spring's blooms flowered hope
yet my summer heart wilted, my will fell flat.

I hide. Grief seeks. Screams
all ye all ye in free as home base disappears.

Grief sets the meter, tempo.
Conducts the slow dirge, demands allegiance.

Late autumn nights shroud my pain.
I plead dawn's light will not break me further.

Our house packed and sold.
Farewell commitments camouflage my loneliness.

I move to an evergreened land
as your voice beckons amid arctic winds.

Snow melts, tundra thaws.
The refrain of your absence blossoms in a new pitch.

I start to stutter, then hum
a first prayer of gratitude. Your love.

Fledgling

to Anchorage in Winter

I am a student again, small and anxious.
The long morning darkness, a blackboard.
The snow, dull chalk. A moose lumbers
across the road, forms my first letters,

left to right. An earthquake shifts to the next
lesson, up and down. Avalanches, falling
rocks, augment the primer. Huge crows
serve as school bells. The air crackles danger.

I arrive from New England where wood-slatted
town centers are centuries old, where nature
appears tame, where hills are soft shadows
on the horizon. Here mountain peaks shape sharp

steep walls. Auroras glow ceilings. My veteran
classmates guide me. They are patient, having
already learned to live with such blatant
vulnerability, for here it cannot be ignored.

I gradually allow the landscape to comfort
my uncertainty, create a cathedral as sunsets
spin stained glass. Increasing spring
light sprouts green in my soul.

Firmament

The moon, my lone
companion, lances the glacial winter sky.

I dream your warm body
spooning mine. Fate foreclosed our future.

Your silent face in silhouette,
a death mask. Wake up, wake up!

A cracked window summons
night's crisp air to cleanse the Reaper's stench.

Absence tolls my time.
I miss your swell breaking over my shore.

I know the moon doesn't sweep the sky.
It's our earth that spins everlasting.

I imagine joining you in the heavens.
As dust, as spirit?

Daylight is too bright. I have become
the night. The stars, your eyes.

TERRY S. JOHNSON recently settled in Anchorage, Alaska, after a lifetime in New England. She performed as a professional harpsichordist before serving as a public school teacher for many years. Her poetry has appeared in numerous journals and anthologies, including *Driftwood, Cancer Poetry Project Anthology, Chest Journal, Edge, Journal of the American Medical Association, Passager, Slipstream, Technoculture,* and *Theodate.* Her collection, *Coalescence,* won a 2014 Honorable Mention in the New England Book Festival, and her second book, *Plunge,* launched in 2019.

www.terrysjohnsonpoet.com

Shanti Arts

Nature · Art · Spirit

Please visit us online
to browse our entire book catalog,
including poetry collections and fiction,
books on travel, nature, healing, art,
photography, and more.

Also take a look at our highly regarded art
and literary journal, *Still Point Arts Quarterly*,
which may be downloaded for free.

www.shantiarts.com

www.ingramcontent.com/pod-product-compliance
Lightning Source LLC
LaVergne TN
LVHW051807080426
835511LV00019B/3435